"Modern people often view the fear of God with disdainful suspicion, but Michael Reeves shows us that godly fear is really nothing other than love for God as God. Reeves also helps us to see that the greatest factor in promoting the fear of God is knowing his grace in Christ. As John Bunyan said, 'There is nothing in heaven or earth that can so awe the heart as the grace of God.' This wonderful book not only teaches but sings, leading us to 'rejoice with trembling' (Ps. 2:11)."

Joel R. Beeke, President and Professor of Systematic Theology and Homiletics, Puritan Reformed Theological Seminary

"We used to sing a hymn that said, 'O how I fear Thee, living God! With deepest, tenderest fears.' No longer. But the hymn's first lines remind us of what we are missing: 'My God, how wonderful Thou art, Thy majesty, how bright.' Only those who find God to be 'wonderful' and his majesty 'bright' experience the 'tenderest' fear. So we have a problem; but thankfully help is at hand in *What Does It Mean to Fear the Lord?* Like an elder brother, Michael Reeves guides us into a fresh understanding of the fear of the Lord. On the way, he introduces us to some of his friends—masters in the school of discipleship—who have walked the path before us. Join him on the journey. You will soon discover why 'the LORD takes pleasure in those who fear him' (Ps. 147:11)."

Sinclair B. Ferguson, Chancellor's Professor of Systematic Theology, Reformed Theological Seminary

"The fear of the Lord is the beginning of wisdom, the Bible says, and reading this book will make you wise—wise to who God is and what God requires of us by way of loving, responsive discipleship. Packed full of historical nuggets, *What Does It Mean to Fear the Lord?* deserves to be widely read. 'Walking in the fear of the Lord' is language that has largely disappeared from the contemporary church. The result is the insipid quality of a great deal of current Christianity. Recapturing the sense of God's incomprehensible greatness and holiness is the needed antidote this book provides. An absolute gem of a book."

Derek W. H. Thomas, Senior Minister, First Presbyterian Church, Columbia, South Carolina; Chancellor's Professor of Systematic and Pastoral Theology, Reformed Theological Seminary

"Ours is a day of great fears—fear of financial collapse, fear of terrorist attacks, fear of climatic disasters, fear of a deadly pandemic—all kinds of fears, except the most important of all: the reverential fear of God. How needed then is this marvelous study of a much-neglected theme, one that is central to the Scriptures and vital to human flourishing."

Michael A. G. Haykin, Chair and Professor of Church History, The Southern Baptist Theological Seminary

"Michael Reeves has given us something we badly need and likely haven't realized—a fresh encounter with the thrilling fear of the Lord. This book will bring renewed devotion and delight. Having read it, I can't wait to read it again!"

Sam Allberry, apologist; Associate Pastor, Immanuel Church, Nashville, Tennessee

WHAT DOES IT MEAN
TO FEAR THE LORD?

Union

A book series edited by Michael Reeves

Rejoice and Tremble: The Surprising Good News of the Fear of the Lord, Michael Reeves (2021)

What Does It Mean to Fear the Lord?, Michael Reeves (2021)

WHAT DOES IT MEAN TO FEAR THE LORD?

MICHAEL REEVES

WHEATON, ILLINOIS

Cover design: Dan Farrell

Cover image: Among the Sierra Nevada, California, by Albert Bierstadt, 1868 (Wikimedia Commons)

First printing 2021

Printed in the United States of America

Scripture quotations are from the ESV® Bible (The Holy Bible, English Standard Version®), copyright © 2001 by Crossway, a publishing ministry of Good News Publishers. Used by permission. All rights reserved.

All emphases in Scripture quotations have been added by the author.

Trade paperback ISBN: 978-1-4335-6536-6

ePub ISBN: 978-1-4335-6539-7

PDF ISBN: 978-1-4335-6537-3

Mobipocket ISBN: 978-1-4335-6538-0

Library of Congress Cataloging-in-Publication Data

Names: Reeves, Michael (Michael Richard Ewert), author.
Title: What does it mean to fear the Lord? / Michael Reeves.
Description: Wheaton, Illinois : Crossway, 2021. | Series: Union | Includes bibliographical references and index.
Identifiers: LCCN 2020027787 (print) | LCCN 2020027788 (ebook) | ISBN 9781433565366 (trade paperback) | ISBN 9781433565373 (pdf) | ISBN 9781433565380 (mobipocket) | ISBN 9781433565397 (epub)
Subjects: LCSH: God (Christianity)—Worship and love. | Fear of God—Christianity.
Classification: LCC BV4817 .R44 2021 (print) | LCC BV4817 (ebook) | DDC 231.7—dc23
LC record available at https://lccn.loc.gov/2020027787
LC ebook record available at https://lccn.loc.gov/2020027788

Crossway is a publishing ministry of Good News Publishers.

VP		30	29	28	27	26	25	24	23	22	21
15	14	13	12	11	10	9	8	7	6	5	4	3	2

For Rob and John, my dear friends

———

In a perfect Friendship this Appreciative Love is, I think, often so great and so firmly based that each member of the circle feels, in his secret heart, humbled before all the rest. Sometimes he wonders what he is doing there among his betters. He is lucky beyond desert to be in such company. Especially when the whole group is together, each bringing out all that is best, wisest, or funniest in all the others. Those are the golden sessions; when four or five of us after a hard day's walking have come to our inn; when our slippers are on, our feet spread out towards the blaze and our drinks at our elbows; when the whole world, and something beyond the world, opens itself to our minds as we talk; and no one has any claim on or any responsibility for another, but all are free-men and equals as if we had first met an hour ago, while at the same time an Affection mellowed by the years enfolds us. Life—natural life—has no better gift to give. Who could have deserved it?

C. S. LEWIS, *The Four Loves*

Contents

Series Preface

OUR INNER CONVICTIONS AND VALUES shape our lives and our ministries. And at Union—the cooperative ministries of Union School of Theology, Union Publishing, Union Research, and Union Mission (visit www.theolo.gy)—we long to grow and support men and women who will delight in God, grow in Christ, serve the church, and bless the world. This Union series of books is an attempt to express and share those values.

They are values that flow from the beauty and grace of God. The living God is so glorious and kind, he cannot be known without being adored. Those who truly know him will love him, and without that heartfelt delight in God, we are nothing but hollow hypocrites. That adoration of God necessarily works itself out in a desire to grow in Christlikeness. It also fuels a love for Christ's precious bride, the church, and a desire humbly to serve—rather than use—her. And, lastly, loving God brings us to share his concerns, especially to see his life-giving glory fill the earth.

Each exploration of a subject in the Union series will appear in two versions: a full volume and a concise one. The concise treatments, such as this one, are like shorter guided tours: they stick to the main streets and move on fast. You may find, at the end of this little book, that you have questions or want to explore some more: in that case, the fuller volume will take you further up and further in.

My hope and prayer is that these books will bless you and your church as you develop a deeper delight in God that overflows in joyful integrity, humility, Christlikeness, love for the church, and a passion to make disciples of all nations.

Michael Reeves

SERIES EDITOR

1

Do Not Be Afraid!

BOO!

It's one of the first words we enjoy. As children, we loved to leap out on our friends and shout it. But at the same time, we were scared of the dark and the monsters under the bed. We were both fascinated *and* repelled by our fears. And not much changes when we grow up: adults love scary movies and thrills that bring us face-to-face with our worst fears. But we also agonize over all the dreadful things that could happen to us: how we could lose our lives, health, or loved ones; how we might fail or be rejected. Fear is probably the strongest human emotion. But it baffles us.

To Fear or Not to Fear?

When we come to the Bible, the picture seems equally confusing: is fear a good thing or bad? Many times Scripture clearly views fear as a bad thing from which Christ has come to rescue us. The apostle John writes: "There is no fear in love, but perfect love casts out fear. For fear has to do with punishment, and whoever fears has not been perfected in love" (1 John 4:18). Indeed, the most frequent command in Scripture is "Do not be afraid!"

Yet, again and again in Scripture we are called to fear. Even more strangely, we are called to fear *God*. The verse that quickly comes to mind is Proverbs 9:10, "The fear of the LORD is the beginning of wisdom." In the New Testament, Jesus describes the unrighteous judge as one "who neither feared God nor respected man" (Luke 18:2). Paul writes, "Let us cleanse ourselves from every defilement of body and spirit, bringing holiness to completion in the fear of God" (2 Cor. 7:1).

All of which can leave us rather confused. On the one hand, we are told that Christ frees us from fear; on the other, we are told we ought to fear—and fear God, no less. It can leave us wishing that "the fear of God" were not so prominent an idea in Scripture. We have enough fears without adding more, thank you very much. And fearing God just feels so negative, it doesn't seem to square with the God of love we meet in the gospel. Why would any God worth loving *want* to be feared?

My aim now is to cut through this confusion. I want you to rejoice in this paradox that the gospel both frees us from fear and gives us fear. It frees us from our crippling fears, giving us instead a most delightful fear. And I want to show that for Christians "the fear of God" really does *not* mean being afraid of God.

Indeed, Scripture will have many hefty surprises in store for us as it describes the fear of God. Take just one example for now. In Isaiah 11:1–3 we are given a beautiful description of the Messiah, filled with the Spirit:

> There shall come forth a shoot from the stump of Jesse,
>   and a branch from his roots shall bear fruit.
> And the Spirit of the LORD shall rest upon him,
>   the Spirit of wisdom and understanding,
>   the Spirit of counsel and might,
>   the Spirit of knowledge and the fear of the LORD.
> And his delight shall be in the fear of the LORD.

Those last two statements should make us question what this fear of the Lord is. Here we see that the fear of the Lord is not something the Messiah wishes to be without. Even he has the fear of the Lord—but he is not reluctant about it. Quite the opposite: his *delight* is in the fear of the Lord. It forces us to ask, what is this fear, that it can be Christ's very delight? It cannot be a negative, gloomy duty.

Today's Culture of Fear

But before we dive into the good news the Bible has about our fears and the fear of God, it is worth noticing how anxious our culture has become. Seeing where our society now is can help us understand why we have a problem with fear—and why the fear of God is just the tonic we need.

These days, it seems, everyone is talking about a culture of fear. From Twitter to television, we fret about global terrorism, extreme weather, and political turmoil. Our private lives are filled with still more sources of anxiety. Take our diet, for example. If you choose the full-fat version on the menu, you're heading for a heart attack. Yet we keep discovering that the low-calorie alternative is actually carcinogenic or harmful in some other way. And so a low-grade fear starts with breakfast. Or think of the paranoia surrounding parenting today. The valid but usually overblown fear of the kidnapper lurking online or outside every school has helped fuel the rise of helicopter parenting and children more and more fenced in to keep them safe. As a whole, we are an increasingly anxious and uncertain culture.

And therein is an extraordinary paradox, for we live more safely than ever before. Though we are safer than almost any other society in history, safety has become the holy grail of our culture. And like *the* Holy Grail, it is something we can never quite reach. Protected like never before, we are skittish and panicky like never before.

How can this be? Quite simply, our culture has lost God as the proper object of fear. That fear of God (as I hope to show) was a happy and healthy fear that controlled our other fears, reining in anxiety. With our society having lost God as the proper object of healthy fear, our culture is necessarily becoming more neurotic and anxious. In ousting God from our culture, other concerns—from personal health to the health of the planet—have assumed a divine ultimacy in our minds. Good things have become cruel and pitiless idols. And thus we feel helplessly fragile, and society fills with anxieties.

The Fearful Legacy of Atheism

The suggestion that loss of the fear of God is the root cause of our culture's anxiety is a real blow to atheism. For atheism sold the idea that if you liberate people from belief in God, that will liberate them from fear. But throwing off the fear of God has not made our society happier and less fretful. Quite the opposite.

So, what does our culture do with all its anxiety? Given its essentially secular self-identity, our culture will not turn to God. The only possible solution, then, must be for us to sort it out ourselves. Thus, Western society has medicalized fear. Fear has become an elusive disease to be medicated. (I do not mean to imply here that use of drugs to curb anxiety is wrong—only that they are a palliative, at times an important one, and not an ultimate solution.)[1] Yet that attempt to eradicate fear as we would eradicate a disease has effectively made comfort (complete absence of fear) a health category—or even a moral category. Where discomfort was once considered quite normal (and quite proper for certain situations), it is now deemed an essentially unhealthy thing.

It means that in a culture awash with anxiety, fear is increasingly seen as *wholly* negative. And Christians have been swept along, adopting society's negative assessment of all fear. Small wonder, then, that we shy away from talking about the fear of God, despite its prominence in Scripture. It is understandable, but it is tragic: the loss of the fear of God is what ushered in our age of anxiety, but the fear of God is the very antidote to our fretfulness.

A Rose by Any Other Name Would Smell as Sweet

The fact is that not all fear is the same, or unhealthy, or unpleasant. We must distinguish between different sorts of fear, between wrong fear and right fear. That is what we will do now. Then we can rejoice in the fact that the fear of God is not like fears that torment us. Then we can appreciate how it is the one positive, wonderful fear that deals with our anxieties.

2

Sinful Fear

WE ALL KNOW FEAR. When you experience fear, your body reacts: you feel the adrenaline release as your heart races, your breathing accelerates, and your muscles tense. Sometimes that can be intensely fun: think of the rush of the roller coaster or the big game. Sometimes it can be terrifying as panic grips you so utterly, you cannot think but only shake, sweat, and fret. Underneath those experiences are common thoughts. Our different fears have common traits, a common DNA.

However, it is important to recognize that there are different *sorts* of fear. Confusion on this point is deadly. Take, for example, how some Christians see the lack of reverence and awe of God in our churches and seem to think the answer is to make people *afraid* of God. As if our love for God needs to be tempered by being *afraid* of him.

Scripture speaks quite differently. Take, for example, Exodus 20, where the people of Israel gather at Mount Sinai:

> Now when all the people saw the thunder and the flashes of lightning and the sound of the trumpet and the mountain smoking, the people were afraid and trembled, and they stood far off and said to Moses, "You speak to us, and we will listen; but do not let God speak to us, lest we die." Moses said to the people, "*Do not fear*, for God has come to test you, *that the fear of him may be before you*, that you may not sin." (vv. 18–20)

Moses here sets out a contrast between being *afraid* of God and *fearing* God: those who have the fear of him will not be afraid of him. Yet he uses the same "fear" word for both. Evidently there is a fear of God that is desirable, and there is a fear of God that is not.

Let's have a look now at the different types of fear of God we meet in Scripture.

Sinful Fear

The first type of fear of God is condemned by Scripture. I have been tempted to call it "wrong fear," but there is a sense in which it is quite right for unbelievers to be afraid of God. The holy God *is* terrible to those who are far from him. Instead, I am calling it "sinful fear," since it is a fear of God that flows from sin.

This sinful fear of God is the sort of fear James tells us the demons have when they believe and shudder (James 2:19). It is the fear Adam had when he first sinned and hid from God (Gen. 3:10). Sinful fear drives you *away* from God. This is the fear of the unbeliever who hates God, who fears being exposed as a sinner and so runs from God.

This is the fear of God that it is at odds with love for God. It is the fear rooted in the very heart of sin. Dreading and retreating from God, this fear generates the doubt that rationalizes unbelief. It is the motor for both atheism and idolatry, inspiring people to invent alternative "realities" in place of the living God. Take, for example, the late Christopher Hitchens, one of the "four horsemen" of the early twenty-first-century "New Atheism." Hitchens preferred to describe himself as an "anti-theist" because he was opposed to the very possibility of God's existence. But this anti-theism, he was clear, was motivated by a fear of God. Asked on Fox News what he thought about the possibility of God's existence, he replied:

> I think it would be rather awful if it was true. If there was a permanent, total, round-the-clock divine supervision and invigilation of everything you did, you would never have a waking or sleeping moment when you weren't being watched and controlled and supervised by some celestial entity from

the moment of your conception to the moment of your death. . . . It would be like living in North Korea.[1]

Hitchens tragically misunderstood God and so feared God.

Misunderstanding God

The experience of Christopher Hitchens shows that this sinful fear that flees from God arises in good part from a misunderstanding of him. The unfaithful servant in Jesus's parable of the ten minas displays exactly this problem when he unfairly complains to his master, "I was afraid of you, because you are a severe man" (Luke 19:21). He sees nothing of his master's kindness: in his shortsighted eyes the great man is all stingy severity, and so the servant is simply afraid.

This is the blindness Satan loves to inflict on our understanding of God. Satan would present God as pure threat. For then, when we perceive God that way, we will run from him in fear.

Yet while this fear drives people away from their Maker, it does not always drive them away from religion. Having presented God as harsh and dreadful, this fear gives people the mindset of a reluctant slave who obeys his master not out of any love but purely from fear of the whip. Out of slavish fear, people will perform all manner of duties to appease a God they secretly despise. To all the world they can seem devout, exemplary Christians, if rather lacking in joy.

The Dread of Holiness

Another part of this sinful fear is the fear of letting go of sin, or what we might call the dread of holiness. C. S. Lewis explored this idea in *The Great Divorce*, a story that starts in the grey town (hell). While everyone there is afraid of the dark, few dare step aboard the bus to heaven, because they are even more afraid of the light. While the darkness shrouds nameless horrors, the light is more scary because it exposes them.

When the bus arrives in the bright beauty of the heavenly meadow, one of the spectral souls from hell screams, "I don't like it. . . . It gives me the pip!"[2] Then the Solid People—the residents of heaven—arrive, at which, Lewis writes, "two of the ghosts screamed and ran for the bus."[3] Their very splendor is terrifying to the shrunken wraiths from hell.

"Go away!" squealed the Ghost. "Go away! Can't you see I want to be alone?"

"But you need help," said the Solid One.

"If you have the least trace of decent feeling left," said the Ghost, "you'll keep away. I don't want help. I want to be left alone."[4]

The fear, for the ghosts, is their realization that to dwell in heaven they must give up their "dignity" or self-dependence, their misery, their anger, their grumbles. They cannot imagine being without the very things that deform them and keep them from happiness, and they shudder at the prospect of liberation and purification. Their fear is a struggle against joy. It is a fear of the light and a refusal to let go of the darkness.

It is the very richness and energy of the pure life of heaven that is so overwhelming and fearful to the ghosts. They will do almost anything to avoid it. Sinners prefer their darkness and chains to the light and freedom of heaven, and so they dread its holiness.

Sinful Fear in Christians

Sadly, Christians are not immune to this sinful fear. Poor teaching, hard times, and Satan's accusations can all feed this cringing fear of God. What weed killer can we use? Really, the rest of this book is an attempt to hold out the deeper cure.

It is the devil's work to promote a fear of God that makes people afraid of God such that they want to flee from God. The Spirit's work is the exact opposite: to produce in us a wonderful fear that wins and draws us *to* God. It is to this happy, Scripture-commended, Spirit-breathed fear that we turn now.

3

Right Fear

C. I. SCOFIELD ONCE CALLED *the fear of God* "a phrase of Old Testament piety."[1] And so it was. However, *the fear of God* is not a phrase of Old Testament piety *only*, for the right fear of God is, quite explicitly, a blessing of the new covenant. Speaking of the new covenant, the Lord promised through Jeremiah:

> And they shall be my people, and I will be their God. I will give them one heart and one way, that they may fear me forever, for their own good and the good of their children after them. I will make with them an everlasting covenant, that I will not turn away from doing good to them. *And I will put the fear of me in their hearts, that they may not turn from me.* (Jer. 32:38–40)

What is this fear that the Lord will put in the hearts of his people? Unlike that devilish fear we have seen that would drive us away from God, this is a fear that keeps us from turning away from him.

An Unexpected Fear

In Jeremiah 33, the Lord goes on to explain this fear in words so striking they overturn all our expectations. He promises:

> I will cleanse them from all the guilt of their sin against me, and I will forgive all the guilt of their sin and rebellion against me. And this city shall be to me a name of joy, a praise and a glory before all the nations of the earth who shall hear of all the good that I do for them. They shall fear and tremble *because of all the good and all the prosperity I provide for it.* (vv. 8–9)

This is not a fear of punishment. Quite the opposite: in Jeremiah 33, the Lord promises to cleanse his people, forgive them, and do great good for them. And they fear and tremble precisely *because of* all the good he does for them.

Here is not a fear that stands on the flip side of the grace and goodness of God. It is the sort of fear Hosea describes when he prophesies how "the children of Israel shall return and seek the LORD their God, and David their king, *and they shall come in fear to the LORD and to his goodness in the latter days*" (Hos.

3:5). It is a fear that, as Charles Spurgeon put it, "leans toward the Lord" *because of* his very goodness.[2]

Take another surprising example of this fear, from when the Lord appears to Jacob at Bethel. Again, the Lord utters not one word of threat but only promise after promise of grace:

> Jacob left Beersheba and went toward Haran. And he came to a certain place and stayed there that night, because the sun had set. Taking one of the stones of the place, he put it under his head and lay down in that place to sleep. And he dreamed, and behold, there was a ladder set up on the earth, and the top of it reached to heaven. And behold, the angels of God were ascending and descending on it! And behold, the LORD stood above it and said, "I am the LORD, the God of Abraham your father and the God of Isaac. The land on which you lie I will give to you and to your offspring. Your offspring shall be like the dust of the earth, and you shall spread abroad to the west and to the east and to the north and to the south, and in you and your offspring shall all the families of the earth be blessed. Behold, I am with you and will keep you wherever you go, and will bring you back to this land. For I will not leave you until I have done what I have promised you." Then Jacob awoke from his sleep and said, "Surely the LORD is in this place, and I did not know

it." And he was afraid and said, "How awesome [fearful] is this place! This is none other than the house of God, and this is the gate of heaven." (Gen. 28:10–17)

The Lord promises to bless and increase Jacob, to be with him and to keep him, never to leave him, and to fulfill all his good purposes for him. And in the face of pure goodness and absolute grace, Jacob *fears*. John Bunyan concluded that this right fear flows primarily

> from a sense of the love and kindness of God to the soul . . . from some sense or hope of mercy from God by Jesus Christ. . . . Indeed nothing can lay a stronger obligation upon the heart to fear God, than sense of, or hope in mercy (Jer 33:8, 9). This begetteth true tenderness of heart, true godly softness of spirit; this truly endeareth the affections to God; and in this true tenderness, softness, and endearedness of affection to God, lieth the very essence of this fear of the Lord.[3]

Fear and Love

Clearly, the fear of God is not at all what we, with our culture's allergic reaction to the concept of fear, might expect. Instead, it is, as Spurgeon said, the "sort of fear which has in it the very essence of love, and without which there would be no joy even in the presence of God."[4] In fact, the closer we look, the closer fear of God and love of God appear. Sometimes fear of God and love of God are put in parallel, as in Psalm 145:

> He fulfills the desire of *those who fear him*;
>> he also hears their cry and saves them.
> The LORD preserves *all who love him*,
>> but all the wicked he will destroy. (vv. 19–20)

The reason it is not obvious to us that fear and love are so alike is that we easily misunderstand love. *Love* is a word bandied around in our lives. I "love" sitting in a cozy armchair reading a good book; I "love" a good laugh with my friends. And so I can blithely assume that "love" for God is just more of the same, meaning nothing more than a (perhaps vague) preference. Where some enjoy pudding, I enjoy God.

However, my love for one thing differs from my love for another because love changes according to its object. Let me illustrate with three true statements:

1. I love and have real affection for my dog.
2. I love and have real affection for my wife.
3. I love and have real affection for my God.

Each is true, but reading them together like that should make you wince. For you know there must be something terribly wrong if I mean exactly the same thing in each. You sincerely hope there is a difference. And there is: the three *loves* differ because the *objects* of the loves differ.

The living God is infinitely perfect and overwhelmingly beautiful in every way. And so we do not love him aright if our love is not a trembling, overwhelmed, and fearful love. In a sense, then, the trembling "fear of God" is a way of speaking about the intensity of our love for God.

The right fear of God, then, is not the flip side to our love for God. Nor is it one side of our reaction to God. It is not that we love God for his graciousness and fear him for his majesty. That would be a lopsided fear of God. We also love him in his holiness and tremble at the marvelousness of his mercy. True fear of God is true love for God defined.

The biblical theme of the fear of God helps us to see the *sort* of love toward God that is fitting. It shows us that God does not want passionless performance or a vague preference for him. To encounter the living God truly means that we cannot contain ourselves. He is not a truth to be known unaffectedly, or a good to be received listlessly. Seen clearly, the dazzling beauty and splendor of God must cause our hearts to quake.

Is *Fear* the Best Word?

So is *fear* the most helpful word for this right response to God? This fear of God is a most positive thing, but it is hard for us to see that, given how negative the word *fear* seems. No wonder Christians prefer words like *awe*, *respect*, and *reverence* in place of *fear*. So, would another word capture it better?

Let's start with one of the words used for fear of God in Scripture. In the Old Testament, the same word can be used for both right and sinful fears: anything from bone-melting dread to ecstatic jubilation. It is used negatively:

> The sinners in Zion are *afraid*;
> trembling has seized the godless. (Isa. 33:14)

And it is used positively: "*They shall fear* and tremble because of all the good and all the prosperity I provide for it" (Jer. 33:9). So, what is the common feature that enables the same word to be used for both experiences? In both verses, the word suggests a physical experience: of weak-kneed trembling, of being staggered. Now, I can tremble in quite different ways. I can shake in terror, as a soldier might under heavy fire. But I can also quake in overwhelmed adoration, as when the bridegroom first sees his bride.

If, then, we are to be faithful to Scripture's presentation of the fear of God, we should use words that encompass that spectrum of positive and negative experience. That helps us see the common feature of those fears: trembling. It shows us that the fear of God is no mild-mannered, reserved, or limp thing. It is a startlingly physical, overpowering reaction. And so, *respect* and *reverence* are simply too weak and grey to stand in as fit synonyms. *Awe* seems a much better fit, though even it doesn't quite capture the physical intensity or the exquisite delight that leans toward the Lord. In fact, these other words can be actively misleading. For example, if we simply use the word *awe*, we will tend to think of fear as a response to only God's transcendence and power, not his graciousness. Or take the word *respect*: it is a strange term for a response to God's love—and so it is an unbalanced substitute for the word *fear*. Similarly, *reverence* can sound too stiff and unresponsive. Not that these are wrong words—it is simply that they are not perfect synonyms for the fear of God.

Perhaps it is best to recognize the shortcomings of all words. The word *fear* has its own baggage, to be sure, but it is well established, and no one word can adequately and completely replace it. If people are to appreciate how the fear of God is distinct from all other fears, synonyms alone will not do: it must be unfolded and taught.

Fear and Joy

Speaking of the happy thrill and exquisite delight of this fear is surprising language. Yet Scripture is clear that just as the fear of God defines true love for God, so it defines true joy in God.

The fear of the Lord is a *pleasure* to believers, for it is about enjoying his fearfully lovely glory.

"Blessed" or "happy"—like God—"is the one who fears the LORD always" (Prov. 28:14). Thus Nehemiah prays, "O Lord, let your ear be attentive to the prayer of your servant, and to the prayer of your servants who *delight to fear your name*" (Neh. 1:11).

This right fear of God is not the gloomy flip side to joy in God. Rather, it is a way of speaking about the sheer intensity of the saints' happiness in God. It helps us to see the *sort* of joy that is most fitting for believers. Our delight in God is not intended to be lukewarm. Our joy in God is, *at its purest*, a trembling and wonder-filled—yes, fearful—joy. For the object of our joy is so fearfully wonderful. We are made to rejoice and tremble before God, to love and enjoy him with an intensity that is fitting for him.

This pairing of joy and fear can be seen when two wise statements are put together. One speaks of "the whole duty of man," the other of "man's chief end," but both are about the purpose for which we were made. The first is from the book of Ecclesiastes where the Preacher concludes: "The end of the matter; all has been heard. Fear God and keep his commandments, for this is the whole duty of man" (Eccles. 12:13). The second statement is the first answer from the Westminster

Shorter Catechism, which tells us, "Man's chief end is to glorify God, and to enjoy him forever." They are describing the same truth. When the Preacher calls us to fear God, he is calling us precisely to the enjoyment of God that Westminster calls the chief end of man.

The nature of the living God means that the fear which pleases him is not a groveling, shrinking fear. He is no tyrant. It is an ecstasy of love and joy that senses how overwhelmingly kind and magnificent, good and true God is, and that therefore leans on him in staggered praise and faith.

4

Overwhelmed by the Creator

THERE ARE DIFFERENT SORTS of fear, then: there is a right fear of God, and there is a sinful fear of God. But there are also different *sorts* of *right* fear of God. There is the fear of God the Creator, and then there is the fear of God the Redeemer in Christ.

"O LORD, How Majestic Is Your Name in All the Earth!"

The first sort of right fear is the trembling response to God as Creator. It appreciates that God is splendid in his transcendence. God is holy, majestic, perfect, all-powerful, and dazzling in all his perfections. This fear considers the Creator and is left staggered, like David, asking, "What is man that you are mindful of him?" (Ps. 8:4). In the light of God's eternal magnificence, self-existence, and unswerving constancy, this fear feels what fleeting and fickle little things we are.

That trembling fear is the right reaction to the Creator. For the holiness of the Creator is not a quiet, anemic thing to be received with stained-glass voices and simpers. The holiness of the sovereign Lord is tremendous, vivid, and dazzling. *Not* to fear him would be blind foolishness. In the splendor of the Creator's majesty, we *should* be abased. In the brightness of his purity, we *should* be ashamed.

Fear of the Creator in Unbelievers

There is a sense in which all people can know *something* of this fear of the Creator. The pantheist poet William Blake (1757–1827) poignantly expressed his fear of God in the words of "The Tyger":

Tyger Tyger, burning bright,
In the forests of the night;
What immortal hand or eye,
Could frame thy fearful symmetry? . . .

And what shoulder, & what art,
Could twist the sinews of thy heart?
And when thy heart began to beat,
What dread hand? & what dread feet? . . .

When the stars threw down their spears
And water'd heaven with their tears:

Did he smile his work to see?
Did he who made the Lamb make thee?[1]

The fearfulness of the tiger leads Blake to consider how dreadful its Creator must be. There is something right there. But Blake can see no further: he is left dreading *but not loving* the Creator.

Fear of the Creator in Believers

Now compare Blake's words with those of the hymn-writer Isaac Watts:

Eternal power, whose high abode
Becomes the grandeur of a God,
Infinite lengths beyond the bounds
Where stars resolve their little rounds.

The lowest step around Thy seat,
Rises too high for Gabriel's feet;
In vain the tall archangel tries
To reach Thine height with wondering eyes.

Thy dazzling beauties whilst he sings,
He hides his face behind his wings,
And ranks of shining thrones around
Fall worshiping, and spread the ground.

Lord, what shall earth and ashes do?
We would adore our maker, too;
From sin and dust to Thee we cry,
The Great, the Holy, and the High!

Earth from afar has heard Thy fame,
And worms have learned to lisp Thy name;
But, O! the glories of Thy mind
Leave all our soaring thoughts behind.

God is in Heaven, and men below;
Be short our tunes, our words be few;
A sacred reverence checks our songs,
And praise sits silent on our tongues.[2]

As with Blake, there is wondering here. But all the tone is different: Watts is full of adoration. His fear is a worshipful and loving fear.

What makes for the difference? Very simply, Watts had been taken further in his knowledge of God. Not only did he have the knowledge of God the Creator; he also had the knowledge of God the Redeemer in Christ. And that knowledge of God as a humble, gracious, and compassionate *Redeemer* beautifies the sight of his transcendent majesty as *Creator*. Our wonder at the Creator's magnificence increases when we know it as the magnificence of the kindest Savior.

Charles Spurgeon argued that while believers have an adoring fear of God, "we, who believe in Jesus, are not afraid of God even as our King."[3] For we know the beautiful *character* of the one who rules: the sovereign Creator is a gracious and merciful Redeemer. Those who are taught only—or even predominantly—that God is King and Creator will be left with William Blake's dread. Only those who also get to hear of God's redeeming graciousness will begin to share Spurgeon's pleasure in his Creator.

> Gazing upon the vast expanse of waters,—looking up to the innumerable stars, examining the wing of an insect, and seeing there the matchless skill of God displayed in the minute; or standing in a thunderstorm, watching, as best you can, the flashes of lightning, and listening to the thunder of Jehovah's voice, have you not often shrunk into yourself, and said, "Great God, how terrible art thou!"—not afraid, but full of delight, like a child who rejoices to see his father's wealth, his father's wisdom, his father's power,—happy, and at home, but feeling oh, so little![4]

Spurgeon was quakingly delighted (and not afraid) because the immensity of the heavens and the complexity of the insects came from "his *father's* wealth, his *father's* wisdom, his *father's* power." He knew the Creator was his Father in Christ.

Overwhelmed by the Father

Filial Fear

"The fear of the Lord is the beginning of knowledge" (Prov. 1:7). It leads us from knowing God as the Creator to knowing him as our Redeemer and Father. By opening our eyes to know God aright, the Spirit turns our hearts to fear him with a loving, *filial* fear. That is the fear that is appropriate for Christians, who are brought by the Son to be beloved, adopted children before their heavenly Father.

Martin Luther knew well how the fatherhood of God changes how we fear God. From his earliest days, Luther had feared God with a loveless dread. As a monk, his mind was filled with the knowledge that God is righteous and hates sin; but Luther failed to see any further into who God is. Not knowing God as a kind and compassionate Father, Luther found he could not love him.

That changed when he began to see that God is a fatherly God. Looking back later in life Luther reflected that, as a monk, he had not actually been worshiping the right God, for it is "not enough," he then said, to know God as the Creator and Judge. Only when God is known as a loving Father is he known aright.

Through sending his Son to bring us back to himself, God has revealed himself to be loving and supremely fatherly. Luther found that not only does that give great assurance and joy—it also wins our hearts to him, for "we may look into His fatherly heart and sense how boundlessly He loves us. That would warm our hearts, setting them aglow with thankfulness."[1] In the salvation of this God we see a God we can wholeheartedly love. Through his redemption our fear is transformed from trembling, slavish terror to trembling, filial wonder.

Jesus's Own Fear

It is Jesus's own filial fear that we are brought to share. Luke's Gospel tells us that as the boy Jesus grew, he "increased in wisdom and in stature" (2:52). Yet the *fear of the Lord is the beginning of wisdom* (Prov. 9:10). Jesus could not have grown in wisdom without the fear of the Lord.

God's great purpose in salvation was that the Son might be "the firstborn among many brothers" (Rom. 8:29), that the Son might share his sonship, bringing us with him before the one we can now enjoy as our Father. This means that not only do believers share the Son's own standing before the Father; we also share the Son's own filial delight in the fear of the Lord.

This filial fear is part of the Son's pleasurable adoration of his Father; indeed, it is the very emotional extremity of that wonder. It is not the dread of sinners before a holy Judge. It is not the awe of creatures before their tremendous Creator. It is the overwhelmed devotion of children marveling at the kindness and glory and complete magnificence of their Father.

That is why it is not *at all* the same thing as being afraid of God. The filial fear the Son shares with us is quite different from the sinner's dread of God. It is an adoration of God.

Why It Matters

Those who do not know God as a merciful Redeemer and compassionate Father can never have the delight of a truly filial fear. At best, they can only tremble at his transcendent awesomeness as Creator. At worst, they can only shudder at the thought that there is a righteous Judge in heaven and hate him in their hearts.

In contrast, those who know that God's holiness is not just his separateness from us sinners in his righteousness or just his separateness from us creatures as Creator but also his absolute incomparability in grace, mercy, and kindness—they see the completeness of the beauty of holiness. They see the most glory.

They see the glory of the cross, the glory of a loving Savior, the glory of a mighty but humble God who is not ashamed to call himself their Father.

It all means that we must keep a careful eye on how we think of God. For the very shape of the gospel we proclaim will tell of how we think of God. Think of the gospel presentation that only describes God as Creator and ruler: sin is no deeper a matter than breaking his rules; redemption is about being brought back under his rulership. Such a gospel could never impart a *filial* fear and wonder, for there is no mention of God's fatherhood or our adoption in his Son. Such a gospel can only leave people with a fear of the Creator.

Only when we are resolutely Christ-centered can we tell a richer, truer gospel. Only then does the story make sense that our sin is a deeper matter than external disobedience, that it is a relational matter of our hearts loving what is wrong. Only then will we speak of God the Father sending forth his Son that he might bring us as children into his family. Only that Christ-centered gospel can draw people to share Jesus's own fear.

When Christians misunderstand the right fear of God as nothing but the fear of the Creator, they rob themselves of their filial fear. It is all too easy to see God's grandeur as Creator—which is absolutely right to do—but then fail to look to the gospel and God's grandeur as a compassionate Savior. In such thinking, God may appear great, but he will not appear good.

Those who know God as Father can have a deeper enjoyment and fear of God. See, for example, how Charles Spurgeon's filial fear of his heavenly Father enriched his wonder at the awesomeness of God as Creator. Spurgeon declared, "I love the lightnings, God's thunder is my delight."

> Men are by nature afraid of the heavens; the superstitious dread the signs in the sky, and even the bravest spirit is sometimes made to tremble when the firmament is ablaze with lightning, and the pealing thunder seems to make the vast concave of heaven to tremble and to reverberate; but I always feel ashamed to keep indoors when the thunder shakes the solid earth, and the lightnings flash like arrows from the sky. Then God is abroad, and I love to walk out in some wide space, and to look up and mark the opening gates of heaven, as the lightning reveals far beyond, and enables me to gaze into the unseen. *I like to hear my Heavenly Father's voice in the thunder.*[2]

Spurgeon could relish the transcendence and creative power of God with a trembling pleasure precisely because he saw them as the transcendence and power not just of a righteous Creator but also of his loving Father. The wonders of creation are best enjoyed by the self-conscious children of God. Lightnings, mountains, stars, and wild oceans are all more marvelous to those who see them all as the works of their majestic and gracious Father.

6

How to Grow in This Fear

THE FEAR OF GOD is not a state of mind you can guarantee with five easy steps. It is not something that can be acquired with simple self-effort. The fear of God is a matter of the heart.

A Matter of the Heart

How easily we can mistake the reality of the fear of God for an outward and hollow show! As Martin Luther put it: "To fear God is not merely to fall upon your knees. Even a godless man and a robber can do that."[1] Scripture presents the fear of God as a matter of the heart's inclinations. So, reads Psalm 112:1,

> Blessed is the man who fears the LORD,
>   who greatly *delights* in his commandments!

The one who fears the Lord, then, is not merely one who grudgingly attempts the outward action of keeping the Lord's commandments. The one who truly fears the Lord greatly delights in God's commandments!

In other words, fear runs deeper than behavior: it *drives* behavior. Sinful fear *hates* God and *therefore* acts sinfully. Right fear *loves* God and therefore has a sincere longing to be like him.

The fear of God as a biblical theme stops us from thinking that we are made for either passionless performance or a detached knowledge of abstract truths. It shows that we are made to know God in such a way that our hearts tremble at his beauty and splendor. It shows us that entering the life of Christ involves a transformation of our very affections, so that we begin actually to despise—and not merely renounce—the sins we once cherished, and treasure the God we once abhorred.

This is why singing is such an appropriate expression of a right, filial fear. "Clap your hands, all peoples!" cry the sons of Korah in Psalm 47;

> Shout to God with loud songs of joy!
> *For the LORD, the Most High, is to be feared.* (vv. 1–2;
>   see also Ps. 96:1–4)

In fact, the fear of the Lord is the reason Christianity is the most song-filled of all religions. It is the reason why, from how

Christians worship together to how they stream music, they are always looking to make melody about their faith. Christians instinctively want to sing to express the affection behind their words of praise, and to stir it up, knowing that words spoken flatly will not do in worship of this God.

How Hearts Change

Since the fear of God is a matter of the heart, how you think you can cultivate it will depend on how you think our hearts work.

Take, for example, Martin Luther. He grew up believing that if you work at outward, righteous acts, you will actually become righteous. However, his experience soon proved that wrong. In fact, he found, trying to sort himself out and become righteous by his own efforts was driving him into a profoundly sinful fear and hatred of God. An outward *appearance* of righteousness he could achieve, but it would be nothing more than a hollow sham.

As Luther saw it, our sinful actions merely manifest whether we love or hate God. Simply changing our habits will not change what we love or hate. What we need is a profound change of heart, so that we want and love differently. We need the Holy Spirit to bring about a fundamental change in us, and he does this through the gospel, which preaches Christ. Only the preaching of Christ can turn a heart to fear God with loving, trembling, filial adoration. Only then, when your heart is turned toward God, will you want to fight to turn your behavior toward him.

"Were You There When They Crucified My Lord? . . . It Causes Me to Tremble"

The cross is the most fertile soil for the fear of God. Why? First, because the cross, by the forgiveness it brings, liberates us from sinful fear. But more than that: it also cultivates the most exquisitely fearful adoration of the Redeemer. Think of the sinful woman with Jesus at the house of Simon the Pharisee: standing at Jesus's feet, "weeping, she began to wet his feet with her tears and wiped them with the hair of her head and kissed his feet and anointed them with the ointment" (Luke 7:38). At this, Jesus said to Simon:

> Do you see this woman? I entered your house; you gave me no water for my feet, but she has wet my feet with her tears and wiped them with her hair. You gave me no kiss, but from the time I came in she has not ceased to kiss my feet. You did not anoint my head with oil, but she has anointed my feet with ointment. Therefore I tell you, her sins, which are many, are forgiven—for she loved much. But he who is forgiven little, loves little. (Luke 7:44–47)

Jesus spoke of her *love*, but the intense physicality of her demonstration of affection fits Scripture's picture of *fear*. Hers was an intensely fearful love. Her love was so intense, it was fearful. When the awesome magnitude of Christ's forgiveness, the extent to which he has gone to atone for us, and therefore the terrible gravity of our sin become clear to us—as they do best at the cross—the right, loving reaction is so intense, it is fearful.

There is another reason the cross is so fertile a soil for the fear of God. For the grace of God serves as a bread-crumb trail, leading us up from the forgiveness itself to the forgiver. In the light of the cross, Christians not only thank God for his grace to us but also begin to praise him for how beautifully kind and merciful he reveals himself to be in the cross. "Oh! that a great God should be a good God," wrote John Bunyan, "a good God to an unworthy, to an undeserving, and to a people that continually do what they can to provoke the eyes of his glory; this should make us tremble."[2]

Bunyan was insistent that the most powerful change of heart toward a true fear of God comes at the foot of the cross. With striking wisdom, Bunyan wrote of how the cross simultaneously cancels the believer's guilt *and* increases our appreciation of just how vile our sinfulness is:

For if God shall come to you indeed, and visit you with the forgiveness of sins, that visit removeth the guilt, but increaseth the sense of thy filth, and the sense of this that God hath forgiven a filthy sinner, will make thee both rejoice and tremble. O, the blessed confusion that will then cover thy face.[3]

It is a "blessed confusion," made of sweet tears, in which God's kindness shown to you at the cross makes you weep at your wickedness. You simultaneously repent and rejoice. His mercy accentuates your wickedness, and your very wickedness accentuates his grace, leading you to a deeper and more fearfully happy adoration of the Savior.

It is not just that we marvel at the forgiveness itself. Left there we could still be full of self-love, not *enjoying* the Savior but *using* him hypocritically as the one who'll get us out of hell free. We are led from the gift to wondering at the glory of the giver, from marveling at what he has done for us to marveling at who he is in himself. His magnanimity and utter goodness undo us and fill us with a fearful and amazed adoration.

7

The Awesome Church

NOW IS A GOOD TIME to put down this book and ask yourself what things you fear. Our fears are highly revealing. What you fear shows what you really love. We fear our children getting hurt because we love them. We fear losing our jobs because we love the security and identity they give us. We fear rejection and criticism because we love approval. Some of these fears are healthy, some are overblown, and some betray deeper sicknesses in our character.

So ask yourself: What do my fears say about me and my priorities, about what I treasure? What do they say about where I am looking for security?

Which do you fear more: being sinful or being uncomfortable? God or man? *Being* a sinner or being *exposed* before others as a sinner?

Our fears are like ECG readings, constantly telling us about the state of our hearts.

So, what does it look like when a believer is filled with a right, filial fear of God? Not a cold, dead, outward, hypocritical *show* of reverential religion, but a heartfelt quaking at the goodness and glory of the Redeemer.

Deeper Communion with God

The fear of the Lord is a heart-level indicator of the warm communion with God that God wants with his children. It is the wondering temperament of those who have been brought to know and enjoy the everlasting mercy of God and who therefore take pleasure in him. Believers who have a right fear of the Lord will bemoan their prayerlessness but will know something of a heartfelt, affectionate prayer life. They will want to know God better and enjoy sweeter and more constant communion with him.

Knowledge and Wisdom

"The fear of the LORD is the beginning of knowledge" (Prov. 1:7). First, the fear of the Lord brings a true knowledge of God, as Creator and as Redeemer, as majestic and as merciful. Any "knowledge of God" that is devoid of such fearful wonder is actually blind and barren. The living God is so wonderful, he is not truly known where he is not heartily adored.

But the fear of the Lord is not only the beginning of knowledge *of God*. It is also the beginning of true knowledge of ourselves. In the light of God's holiness and majesty I understand how puny, vicious, and pathetic I am. In other words, I do not have a true knowledge of myself if I do not fear God. Without that fear, my self-perception will be wildly distorted by my pride. It is when we are most thrilled with God that our masks slip and we see ourselves for what we really are: creatures, sinners, forgiven, adopted.

The fear of the Lord is also the beginning of wisdom (Prov. 9:10). But it is a very unexpected guide to wisdom. When we look for wisdom, we look to *intelligence*. We struggle to distinguish between intelligence and wisdom. Which is odd, given how the world is littered with clever fools. We need the fear of God to steer our abilities, and without it, all our abilities are a liability. Take the brilliant young theological thug online: he may just be as bright as he thinks he is, but his untempered ability only makes him more dangerous.

And therein lies a challenge for those conscious of their own ability, and a comfort for all who feel daunted by the talents of others. It is only this wonderful fear of God that can steer us wisely through life. This—not IQ—is the beginning of wisdom. Therefore, says Psalm 115:13,

he will bless those who fear the LORD,
  both the small and the great.

For it is not talent that God blesses so much as the fear of God.

Becoming like God

Those who fear God become like him. For, like a fire in the heart, the fear of the Lord consumes sinful desires, and it fuels holy ones. It brings us to *adore* God and so loathe sin and long to be truly like him.

Becoming like God must mean becoming happy. God, after all, is "the blessed" or happy God (1 Tim. 1:11). You naturally expect that the fear of God would make you morose and stuffy, but quite the opposite. Unlike our sinful fears, which make us gloomy, the fear of God has a profoundly uplifting effect: it makes us happy. How can it not when it brings us to know this God?

Along with making us happy, the fear of the Lord makes believers large-hearted, like God. Think of the little story of the prophet Obadiah:

Now the famine was severe in Samaria. And Ahab called Obadiah, who was over the household. (Now Obadiah feared the LORD greatly, and when Jezebel cut off the prophets of the LORD, Obadiah took a hundred prophets and hid them

by fifties in a cave and fed them with bread and water.)
(1 Kings 18:2–4)

Far from making Obadiah self-involved and frosty, the fear of God made him generous and compassionate to those hunted prophets in need.

That large-heartedness is actually the overflow of a tender-heartedness toward God. It means that those who fear God have—to use another much-misunderstood word—a jealousy for God. Such righteous jealousy should not be confused with selfish envy: it is a love that will not let go of the beloved or make do with substitutes. As God the Father is jealous for his beloved Son, and as Christ is jealous for his bride, the church, so too those who fear God find in themselves a loving jealousy for God. Adoring him, they cannot abide his glory being diminished or stolen. False teaching will distress them, not because it contradicts their views but because it impugns *him*. Self-righteousness becomes loathsome to them because of how it steals from the glory of his grace.

From this grows another Christlike quality: humility. "So do not become proud, but fear," wrote Paul (Rom. 11:20), for trembling in wonder at God keeps one from trusting in oneself. It is the key to true humility, which is not about trying to think less of yourself or trying to think of yourself less but about marveling more at him. It is *the* antidote to pride and the prayerlessness that springs from pride. When God is so marvelous in our eyes that we rejoice and tremble, we cannot but praise him and throw ourselves on him in hearty and dependent prayer. We cannot be great in our own eyes. Not only that, but this fear levels and unites us as a church. This fear admits no boasting before God and so admits no elite and no second-class in the church. It also gathers us together in the warm and humble fellowship of a shared love.

Finding Strength

The fear of the Lord also gives believers strength, especially in the face of anxieties and the fear of man. We don't tend to talk much about "the fear of man" today: we call it people-pleasing or peer pressure. Classic signs of it are the overcommitment that comes from an inability to say no, self-esteem issues, and an excessive sensitivity to the comments and views of others. And need I even mention our fear of evangelism?

So *how* can the fear of the Lord free us from our anxieties and our fear of man? Essentially, it acts like Aaron's staff, which ate up the staffs of the Egyptian magicians. As the fear of the Lord grows, it eclipses, consumes, and destroys all rival fears. So the Lord could advise Isaiah: "*Do not fear what they fear*, nor be in dread. But the LORD of hosts, him you shall honor as holy. *Let him be your fear*, and let him be your dread" (8:12–13). When the fear of the Lord becomes central and most important, other fears subside.

Here is truth for every Christian who needs the strength to rise above his or her anxieties, or who needs the strength to pursue an unpopular but righteous course. The fear of the Lord is the only fear that *imparts* strength. And the strength this fear gives is—uniquely—a *humble* strength. Those who fear God are simultaneously humbled *and* strengthened before his beauty and magnificence. Thus they are kept gentle and preserved from being overbearing in their strength.

All of us are temperamentally inclined to lean one way or another. Some are natural rhinos: strong and thick-skinned, but not gentle. Others are more like deer: sweet and gentle, but nervous and flighty. The fear of the Lord corrects and beautifies both temperaments, giving believers a gentle strength. It makes them—like Christ—simultaneously lamblike and lionlike.

The Battle of Fears in the Christian Life

Since fear is a matter of the heart, reorienting our fears is no easy, quick matter. And we have an enemy whose spiteful aim is to make us afraid of God and afraid of everything, who would have us sulk and tremble. But reorienting our fears and affections is a daily battle we must join.

Left to our sinful fears of God, we will shrink from God in guilt and not enjoy his goodness. Left to our fear of man, we will wilt before every criticism, unable to enjoy real fellowship. And just as a right and happy fear of God is fostered by the truth, sinful fears grow in a bed of Satan's lies. We must counter with the truth that drives out anxiety. Into the battlefield of our troubled hearts we send the promises of God. Safe in Christ, we testify to ourselves afresh that the Almighty is our compassionate Redeemer and loving Father, and that he is able, willing, and near to us as we call on him.

In the face of our culture of anxiety, having this right fear of God will beautifully adorn and attest to the reality of the gospel we proclaim. Thereby we can give the lie to the atheist claim that liberating ourselves from the fear of God will make a less fearful culture. Quite the opposite: we can show that this fear—which is pleasurable and not disagreeable—is precisely what can liberate us from the anxieties now flooding our culture.

Sharing God's Fearsomeness

In Song of Solomon, the bridegroom makes a statement about his bride that is eye-catching:

> You are beautiful as Tirzah, my love,
>> lovely as Jerusalem,
>> awesome as an army with banners. . . .

Who is this who looks down like the dawn,
    beautiful as the moon, bright as the sun,
    awesome as an army with banners? (6:4, 10)

The bride is like an army. And she is bright like the sun, with the reflected beauty of the moon. She has become *awesome*. That is true of the church, which is the bride of Christ: the church comes to reflect the bridegroom's awesome magnificence. We know from the apostle Paul that believers are being transformed into the image of Christ (2 Cor. 3:18). But Song of Songs specifies that that transformation is a growth in *reflected awesomeness*.

Led by the Spirit into conformity with Christ, the church begins to exhibit to the world fearsome divine qualities of holiness, happiness, wholeness, and beauty. Thus the church shines like the moon in the darkness, eliciting both wonder and dread. Believers become like heaven's Solid People in Lewis's *The Great Divorce*: their very wholeness and loving joyfulness are fearful to others. This combination is deeply alluring and inexplicable, yet at the same time troubling to unbelievers for how it exposes their grumbling crookedness. In the fear of God, believers become—like their God—blessedly and beautifully fearsome.

8

Eternal Ecstasy

IN THE PRESENCE OF THE LORD, everyone trembles. Before him, Abraham, Joshua, David, Ezekiel, Daniel, Paul, and John all fell on their faces. But it is not just people who tremble. In Isaiah's vision of the Lord enthroned in the temple, "the foundations of the thresholds shook at the voice of him who called" (6:4). And it doesn't stop there: at his appearing,

> the mountains quake before him;
>> the hills melt;
> the earth heaves before him,
>> the world and all who dwell in it. (Nah. 1:5)

Just so, all things will shake and tremble at the second coming of Christ. At Sinai "his voice shook the earth, but now he has promised, 'Yet once more I will shake not only the earth but also the heavens'" (Heb. 12:26). But what sort of trembling is this that will grip the universe? For the heavens and the earth, it is clearly a trembling of exultation. The earth shakes with pleasure, for it is joining in with the joy of believers as their filial fear swells with delight at the presence of their God.

> For the creation waits with eager longing for the revealing of the sons of God. For . . . the creation itself will be set free from its bondage to corruption and obtain the freedom of the glory of the children of God. For we know that the whole creation has been groaning together in the pains of childbirth until now. (Rom. 8:19–22)

On that last day, the glory of the Lord will fill the earth, and his people will fall down in fearsome wonder, delight, and praise.

Yet, at the same appearance of the Lord in glory, the sinful fear of unbelievers will swell into a horrified dread as they hide "themselves in the caves and among the rocks of the mountains, calling to the mountains and rocks, 'Fall on us and hide us from the face of him who is seated on the throne, and from the wrath of the Lamb, for the great day of their wrath has come, and who can stand?'" (Rev. 6:15–17). Where the final appearing of the Lord in glory fills believers with an unprecedented joyful fear of the Redeemer, it fills unbelievers with a new level of dread at their Judge.

That day will usher in a new age in which both the sinful fears of unbelievers and the right fear of believers will crescendo. Both sorts of fear will climax and become eternal states—an ecstasy of terror, on the one hand, and delight, on the other.

Hell Is a World of Fear

Hell—the destiny of all unbelievers—will be a dreadful place. Death is "the king of terrors" (Job 18:14), and hell will be the place of eternal death. It will be the ultimate sump of all sinful fears, heaving with a shared dread of holiness. There, like the demons who believe and shudder (James 2:19), its occupants will hate God and the exposing light of his glory. Sin first made the world a place full of fear, and hell is its culmination: a place of unrelieved fears, and of sinful fear come to a head.

Heaven Is a World of Fear

Where hell is the dreadful sewer of all sinful fears, heaven is the paradise of unconfined, maximal, delighted *filial* fear. "The pillars of heaven tremble" (Job 26:11). Why? For it is the dwelling place of

> a God greatly to be feared in the council of the holy ones,
>> and awesome above all who are around him. (Ps. 89:7)

And as the radiant angels now fall on their faces in fearful, ecstatic joy and adoration before God, so one day will all the saints.

Nothing Else to Fear

Because we tend today to think of fear as a wholly negative thing, it jars us to think of fear remaining in heaven. To be sure, in heaven there will no longer be anything of which to be *afraid*. There the children of God will finally be out of reach of all danger. There will be no fear of punishment, nor any trace of any sinful fear of God left in us. We will rejoice to know him as he is, with no distortion, no misunderstanding, and no devilish whispers of doubt.

Instead, our clear apprehension of God will then enhance our wondering, trembling adoration. Not afraid of anything, the saints will be caught up into God's own fearful happiness and will be overwhelmed by exultation in the glory of God. In other words, our eternal joy will consist precisely in this fear of God: rejoicing and marveling so entirely that, like the angels, we tremble and fall on our faces in wonder.

Like Flames of Fire

Today, we don't often speak of the emotional intensity of what our experience will be in heaven. But Scripture is clear that to be in the presence of God will give us not a tepid happiness, but a quaking, fearfully overwhelmed, ecstatic pleasure.

We get an appetizer of this heavenly and perfected filial fear in this life when we sing heartily in worship together.

> Shout to God with loud songs of joy!
> For the LORD, the Most High, is to be feared. (Ps. 47:1–2)

We catch its scent when the gospel, the Scriptures, or even some beauty in creation makes us well up or drop to our knees in sweet adoration. That overwhelmed sense when our bodies react unbidden to the strength of our affection is a small preview of the day when we will fall at our Lord's feet, too full of joy to stand.

In fact, all fears are a foretaste. The sinful fears and dreads of unbelievers are the firstfruits of hell; the filial fears of Christians are the firstfruits of heaven. Now our fears are partial; then they will be unconfined. For now, Christians see in part, and so we love and rejoice only in part. We hang our heads knowing that moments of filial, trembling wonder are all too faint and all too few. But when we see him as he is, that ecstasy will be unimpaired and absolute.

Yet, even now the Spirit is enlivening believers. From the moment of regeneration, when he breathes new life into a soul, the Spirit's work is to move us from spiritual lethargy to vivaciousness. And that is precisely all about growth in the fear of the Lord. To fear the Lord is to be more *alive*; it is for our love, joy, wonder, and worship of God to be more acute and affecting. When we rejoice in God so intensely that we quake and tremble, then are we being most heavenly.

The Expulsive Power of a Filial Fear

Perhaps the most famous sermon ever delivered in the historic pulpit of the Tron Church in Glasgow was Thomas Chalmers's "The Expulsive Power of a New Affection." In it he argued that nobody can "dispossess the heart of an old affection, but by the expulsive power of a new one."[1] His point was that we cannot simply will ourselves to love God more; the love of sin can be expelled only by the love of God. Chalmers could have been speaking of fear, for it is the ultimate affection and the very aroma of heaven. It is the affection that expels our sinful fears and our anxieties. It is the affection that expels spiritual lethargy. To grow in this sweet and quaking wonder at God is to taste heaven now.

Notes

Chapter 1: Do Not Be Afraid!

1. For a perceptive introduction to this issue, see Michael R. Emlet, "Prozac and the Promises of God: The Christian Use of Psychoactive Medication," desiringGod (website), August 22, 2019, https://www.desiringgod.org/articles/prozac-and-the-promises-of-god.

Chapter 2: Sinful Fear

1. Christopher Hitchens, interview on *Hannity & Colmes*, Fox News, May 13, 2007.
2. C. S. Lewis, *The Great Divorce* (London: Geoffrey Bles, 1946; repr., London: Fount, 1997), 17.
3. Lewis, *The Great Divorce*, 18.
4. Lewis, *The Great Divorce*, 46–47.

Chapter 3: Right Fear

1. *Scofield Reference Bible*, 1909 ed., 607n1.
2. C. H. Spurgeon, "A Fear to Be Desired," in *The Metropolitan Tabernacle Pulpit Sermons*, 63 vols. (London: Passmore & Alabaster, 1855–1917), 48:495.

3. John Bunyan, "A Treatise on the Fear of God," in *The Works of John Bunyan*, ed. George Offer, 3 vols. (Glasgow: W. G. Blackie & Son, 1854; repr., Edinburgh: Banner of Truth, 1991), 1:460–61.

4. Spurgeon, "A Fear to Be Desired," 494.

Chapter 4: Overwhelmed by the Creator

1. William Blake, "The Tyger" (1794).

2. Isaac Watts, "Eternal Power, Whose High Abode" (1706).

3. C. H. Spurgeon, "A Fear to Be Desired," in *The Metropolitan Tabernacle Pulpit Sermons*, 63 vols. (London: Passmore & Alabaster, 1855–1917), 48:498.

4. Spurgeon, "A Fear to Be Desired," 496.

Chapter 5: Overwhelmed by the Father

1. *Luther's Large Catechism* (St. Louis, MO: Concordia, 1978), 70.

2. *C. H. Spurgeon's Autobiography, Compiled from His Diary, Letters, and Records, by His Wife and His Private Secretary*, vol. 1, *1834–1854* (Chicago: Curts & Jennings, 1898), 205, my emphasis.

Chapter 6: How to Grow in This Fear

1. Martin Luther, *Luther's Works*, vol. 51, *Sermons I*, ed. Jaroslav Jan Pelikan, Hilton C. Oswald, and Helmut T. Lehmann (St. Louis, MO: Concordia, 1999), 139.

2. John Bunyan, "The Saints' Knowledge of Christ's Love," in *The Works of John Bunyan*, ed. George Offer, 3 vols. (Glasgow: W. G. Blackie & Son, 1854; repr., Edinburgh: Banner of Truth, 1991), 2:14.

3. John Bunyan, "A Treatise on the Fear of God," in *The Works of John Bunyan*, 1:440.

Chapter 8: Eternal Ecstasy

1. Thomas Chalmers, "The Expulsive Power of a New Affection," in *Posthumous Works of the Rev. Thomas Chalmers*, vol. 6 (New York: Harper & Brothers, 1848–1850), 253.

Scripture Index

Union

We fuel reformation in churches and lives.

Union Publishing invests in the next generation of leaders with theology that gives them a taste for a deeper knowledge of God. From books to our free online content, we are committed to producing excellent resources that will refresh, transform, and grow believers and their churches.

We want people everywhere to know, love, and enjoy God, glorifying him in everything they do. For this reason, we've collected hundreds of free articles, podcasts, book chapters, and video content for our free online collection. We also produce a fresh stream of written, audio, and video resources to help you to be more fully alive in the truth, goodness, and beauty of Jesus.

If you are hungry for reformational resources that will help you delight in God and grow in Christ, we'd love for you to visit us at unionpublishing.org.

unionpublishing.org

Also Available
from Michael Reeves

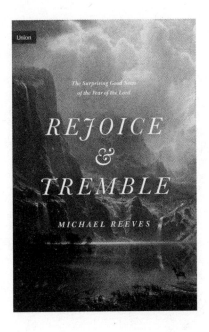

Michael Reeves brings clarity where there is confusion as he encourages us to rejoice in the strange paradox that the gospel both frees us from sinful fear and leads us to godly fear.

For more information, visit **crossway.org**.